D1714654

Blue Tile

Nicola Vulpe

BuschekBooks

Library and Archives Canada Cataloguing in Publication

Vulpe, Nicola, 1954–
      Blue tile / Nicola Vulpe.

Poems.
ISBN 1-894543-22-X

     I. Title.

PS8593.U55B58 2004   C811'.54   C2004-904452-4

Cover image from star-shaped overglaze leaf-gilded tile in the style of Takht-e Solaiman, 13th–14th century (ceramic) by Islamic School, used with permission from Reza Abbasi Museum, Tehran, Iran/Bridgeman Art Library.
Cover design by Dave Boynton.
Typeset in 10 point Bembo.
Printed by Hignell Book Printing, Winnipeg, Manitoba, Canada.

BuschekBooks gratefully acknowledges the support of the Canada Council for the Arts for its publishing program.

BuschekBooks
PO Box 740535
5 Beechwood Avenue
Ottawa K1M 2H9 Canada
buschek.books@sympatico.ca

Canada Council
for the Arts

Conseil des Arts
du Canada

for Maha & Lulu

Contents

Spanish Notebook

Two Men, Honest and True

They were so near I never knew quite
who was the squire, who the knight

One was lettered, the other not,
the noble hidalgo and his man
wandering as one the hard face of Spain

One travelled for love, and honour and fame,
the other for spoils and a kingdom his own,
but glad for a night at the inn,
soup and clean straw and wine

One simple and stout, one mad,
on donkey and nag
—and all the windmills of Spain

O Rocinante! O Sancho!
O Dulcinea and all the saints!
This journey is long indeed

One was the hero, the other the friend;
they had adventures, and died in the end

Hendaya

... or perhaps it was we simply left
rubbing our eyes against the sudden sun, wondering
—now that we had crossed the river—
what it was, exactly, that would be different,
what it was that would not be the same

And lugged our bags across the tracks
and added ourselves to the untidy queue
and shuffled and scratched and yawned
and stared at nothing in particular

We watched the guard's blue eyes, and his hand,
and read the visas with him,
followed the stamp onto the page ...

And took our passports back at last
and thumbed them once again

"Hendaya," they read, "Hendaya"

... or perhaps it was I went to the bar to seek out coffee
and came back with some strange breakfast things

... or the unfamiliar coins we fingered as we sat

We drained our cups, we checked our watches,
made immaterial adjustments once again

... or was it something we did that morning
or something else—

The long night through France
or the rain and yellow lights at Austerlitz
or the old, stale smell of train we could not shake

… or something we did not do

But something there was in that station
that concluded

As though the world behind the river now
was closed

… or had never been

CÓRDOBA

This being Córdoba, you've every right to expect
    the Great Mosque, Maïmonides
    a borrowed lament for the decline of Islam
    and the expulsion of the Jews

At the very least Lorca
    oranges and olive groves and guitars

But this being Córdoba,
    I can only tell you how cold it was, how dark
    and how we bluffed our way about the streets
    looking for a place to feed the poet
    and the ambassador

How we doubled back—twice—and were glad
    they understood less Spanish than they thought

We lighted at last on a suitable place

And this being Córdoba they both chose fish:
    the one haddock, the other hake
    and laid back the wine

The one preferred red, the other rosé
    and demanded the resurrection of tradition

The first loathed tourists, and had no dessert

And this being Córdoba there was a Basque girl,
    as foreign as ourselves

And the walk back was confusing and lonely

But this being Córdoba
    we made arrangements for their breakfasts
    then saw them to their rooms, the poet
    and the ambassador

And ourselves to ours

And this being Córdoba
    in the morning at the AVE
    I bought a paper and a guidebook

And this being Córdoba
    in the year 900 Abbas ben Farras
    learned the secret of glass

And the year following came to grief
    with his flying machine of feathers and wind
    at the foot of the great tower
    guarding the Guadalquivir

CÁDIZ

I remember especially
the surprising green of the prickly pears,
the aluminum pans,
and how in that heat
he wore a beret

We could go no farther

We found water
and grateful for the shade
wound our way back
through the rectangular streets

Shopkeepers were pulling down shutters for the long noon

We passed the dragon tree, and the square
where I'd had dinner with Marisa

(I said nothing of this to you,
—it was unimportant at the time—
and tried to remember something from de Falla,
because this, I read on a plaque, was where he was born)

We peered into a courtyard, the door ajar
and discussed briefly the Arab origin of the tiles

And noticed suddenly
the streets were empty

We plodded on to the ramparts and set out along the paseo
clockwise, as I remember

(There is too much light, I thought
too much, and no colour)

We had walked there that morning
and the evening before,
and the morning before that

And we walked there again,
stopping to share out the fruit

I remember, while we ate, the boys
barefoot on the boulders below
squabbling over a fish one had hauled in,
scrambling like crabs and spitting

And beyond,
white sails—a tanker hulking in from Canarias,

    cold Atlantic
    and America

At the End of Triana

At the end of Triana
the paseo folds into a barranco

On one side the sea
on the other the mountain
and the road pulling up to Tafira

At the end of Triana
beyond the shoe shops, the cafés and boutiques

Beyond the news-stands, the bookstore
and Don Fernando's—
the best ice-cream in town

At the end of Triana
where local events of cultural note
are occasionally held

A step from the Opera
where minks are de rigueur in spite of the heat

Where outside a Cuban quartet
serenades late drinkers for tips

At the end of Triana
where begging is not allowed

Where lovers stroll into the Atlantic night

At the end of Triana
if you turn right when facing the sea

Before the barranco, the market
and the house of Columbus

Near the fork in the paseo,
just prior to the road and the sea-wall,
at the end

Where the shadows are darker
and the facades a little more worn

At the end of Triana,
in spite of everything

there is a monument
to Juan Negrín

DE FALLA AT THE POLICE STATION

Don Manuel, with all due respect,
these are rumours, and rumours as you know
are usually lies

Things are confused, the country's a mess,
but leave that to us, Don Manuel,
we'll fix things up in a snap

No one's been arrested
No one's been shot,
certainly not your friend—
Federico you said his name was?

You may file a complaint if you like,
but sometimes a man just decides, Don Manuel,
not to come home

And politics, Don Manuel,
is a dangerous indulgence
for a poet
or,
with all due respect,
even a musician

GUERNICA

We pulled off the highway and followed the signs
and looked about carefully as we rolled through the town

There had been disagreement
on the importance of stopping

With Vitoria before us
and Burgos and Sahagún and a long way to León

Six hours more and the roads not good,
so we rolled through the town,
peered through the rain

There must be a museum
there must be a monument
there must be a plaque—

Old men in front of a café
wearing berets in the fashion of the Basque,
not flopped to the side but pointed in front

What did you expect?—

We turned a block
and found ourselves where we had begun

And rolled out of the valley onto the road

And were gone

Orwell's Dream

Orwell's dream as he squatted, his testicles ravaged by lice, shivering and sweating in the trenches, was not what you imagine, was not the Monolith, was not the Pig Farm, was not Big Brother, the Ministry of Love, Days of Hate, was none of these; these came later, after the fall, after the Republic, after the undecision, the decision, defeat; he dreamt of coffee, of sitting on the plaza, of sipping coffee in Huesca

Osca to the Romans, heart of another republic 2,000 years buried, another civil war, another front, another undecision; not the same men but the same vermin—and defeat

Huesca, on the far side of the front, beyond the gully, the barbed-wire; behind the Army of Africa, the machine-guns squirting fear and the future, the trenches, the supply roads and the lines of command laid out upon Europe and beyond—and the world playing ostrich

Huesca, had you fallen—now, a half century on, you, fellow dreamer, drink this coffee with me, belated victory, indistinct as a watershed, indelible as a river; give a moment of silence for the fallen of Aragón, Catalonia, for Orwell and his ministries; and those who made them and unmade them; and, discretely, check your testicles: parasites are stubborn things, they have a habit of returning

ATTILA JÓZSEF'S LAST POEM

Attila József's last poem
before he tossed his carcass to a train

Attila József's last poem
gleaned from a headline—
How did he know?

A small town in Spain,
a small town in the north,
a mile from the river,
a mile from the border:
the fall of Irun

How did he know?
How did he see?
gleaned from a headline—
the fall of Irun:

The beetle-headed armies,
tattoo guns at ready

Attila József, his last poem,
the crashing wheels of a freight

BRUNETE

I did not go to Brunete

The driver said it was too far,
I would be late, and who
did I know there—in Brunete—
anyway?

I would be late.
I had an interview and lunch,
someone was waiting
—interested, she said she was—
to size me up

I could go to Brunete
but I would be late

I found myself with three:
One said "Aye", the other "Nay",
the third had no opinion to express

The sun was clear,
but somehow I remember
the food as indifferent,
and everything around as brown,
like tired sand, or mud

A long day it'd been

I waited for a bus to drag me back
through flat, grey suburbs to Madrid

A last sign called as we turned into a street,
white with black letters:
"Brunete," it said

I did not go
I was tired
It was late
It did not matter

The dead there did not need
a tourist or a poet
to resurrect their pain

a dusty afternoon in August
from tired sand, or mud

LETTER FROM THE MÁLAGA ROAD

It's not that the telephone's down, the world cut away,
shells whistling in as yet another Heinkel
circles,
then stoops for a run at the road

It's not that old women
have laid down their bundles, their carcasses,
children stumbled off into the stones

that soldiers have dropped their rifles,
and run

It's none of all that, Beth

It's 1996 now, the sky is clear, the horizon
pale yellow, silent,

the only plane's an Airbus
pencilling an arc out across
the Mediterranean

and in the valleys behind, the olive trees
reach patiently for the sun

No, it's none of all that

It's not that this city left wide open is burning,
that the generals are boozing in Valencia—

that one truck and a handful of dreamers and believers
cannot redeem them

It's that here, Beth,
here with no news since I can recall,
no news from beyond the din and the dust,
the litter and the old, worming passions

in this peace, as it's called,
I have learned, too,
how a man determined might drink
or work his way

blazing

into darkness

THIS SAME WAR ONCE AGAIN
for the Mac-Paps

O young men! O you women in your minks!
as you race on in your wax-red Mercedes,
the tops down, the wind
tearing at your California coiffes, the sun
playing off the gold trinkets you collect
as a matter of course—

O once comrades!
as you speed headlong into tomorrow,
O once can you not slow your flight?—
not long, just long enough
to set your slavering muzzles to the earth—
no, not long, just enough
to sniff at our poor-men's graves?

Even a dog would do more

O Spaniards!
After all, we have lain here a good generation and some
The danger is past, we are but bones

O Spain!
Here we learned the worth of our dreams

And we lost

FOR SEÑOR LAYTON
who, it seems, was a poet and piqued
over an affair of cheese

You come, sir, your pockets stuffed with cash
half across the world without a haircut
or a decent suit

Shabbier than a day-jobber or a Gypsy,
with all those dollars or pounds or marks
you won't pay ten duros for a decent meal
but come to me for a snack,
and want it cheap

You count out the pesetas, sir,
I'll weigh up the cheese

If with your money and bad manners
you choose to eat with pigeons in a park,
do not fancy yourself Cervantes or Quevedo,
and spend your bile on me

You count out the pesetas, sir,
I'll weigh up the cheese

HALF-DAY IN MADRID

It was a different place we left,
jet fuel rubbing in our throats, and cold;
the red-grey hills beyond, the mountains
and precise blue sky

We'd arrived at dawn
tried out the metro, found a bar
somewhere near a familiar station—

What was it we'd done here years ago?

Hung about while three waiters
elbowed each other for a chance
to coax our child to eat

And already it was mid-morning—
we should have planned another day, a week—
the Prado, the Reina Sofía,
the Puerta del Sol with the papers, the hawkers
the tourists
and occasional thief

The cab driver from Jaén
who didn't know a single street
but smiled and smiled and blessed his map
and the Virgin at every light

And green-eyed Mini
stepped pristine from a Velásquez
into her bar no wider than a door

And Pablo, her Sancho
And a hundred other things—

The eels at that exquisite place
—what was it called?—with all the wood,
where writers and revolutionary dandies
dragged the last century to its end

Our friends at Espronceda,
and people we'd not write to when we'd gone—

But that was that

The rest in an airport lounge,
stumbling over luggage to pay for coffee,
thumbing our passports ...

The Price of Transmigration

A BOOK, THE WIND

In Genoa, it's no longer raining

A priest in his cassock hurries,
a book tucked under his arm,
there on the mountain
at the edge of discovery

A red ribbon flutters from the book's cover
"Best of Show", "1st Prize" it says in gold letters,
but in Italian

Not his, not the priest's,
but Voronezhski's *Lirika*,
a book I've just invented—

"The East wind,
not the South but the East,
teases the sea"

"The ships are below us,
idle at their moorings"

The wind tugs at the cassock, at the ribbon,
the priest clutches the book

On whose pages somewhere
someone has noted in a margin

"In the cave in the mountain
at the centre of darkness
we seek only darkness"

WHY MIDDLE MANAGERS NEED POETRY
for Russell Smith, d. 1999

Because there isn't really time

Because we're overworked and overpaid
and can't quite remember anymore
what it is we do

Because we're a favoured consumer profile
but haven't the time

We accumulate airmiles and accessories
some even in real leather

Because we breakfast with strangers
who use our first names

Because we work late

Because we believe in our destiny and our duty
and haven't the time
to reflect or believe or to question

We just make decisions
and live, and die by the consequences

Because we promise ourselves a thousand things

Because we've always wanted to be potters or poets
but stuck with the project to the end

Because we will be better
and are busier

Because we are jealous of greater success
and hate ourselves for not being more clever

We are not indifferent
just not particularly ambitious

Because we drink
and call up past lives and cannot sleep
after they have hung up

Because we make love selfishly
and say we didn't and can't understand
why you say it isn't the same anymore

Because there isn't time

Because we've finally understood
that it doesn't really matter

Tomorrow we'll be fired
—or promoted

Probably we'll be fired

Because we're overworked and overpaid
Because our children could care less
Because there isn't time

Because Russell Smith

is dead

EPITAPH FOR A GOOD CANADIAN
A Poem from the Nasty Nineties

First they went after the railroads
and I didn't mind
I'd never much liked unions
and I had my car

Then they went after the Post Office
—a rusted old tricycle on the information highway—
and that was fine
I had my phone

Then they went after the teachers
and that was fine too
I never needed much school, why should the kids?

Then they went for the CBC
and there was a protest
but it was Super Bowl Weekend
and I was tired

And I had cable, and anyway
the game's not been the same
since Gretzky went to L.A.

And they went for the arts
and I liked that
and science and research, who needs it?
the Yanks and the Japs do it all anyway

And there were the civil servants
I was tired of taxes—who isn't?
so I liked that too

And they stuck it to the hospitals
the doctors packed, so did the nurses

And that was okay
I wasn't sick

And I wasn't old and I had my savings
so I said nothing when they hacked at the pensions
and I had a job, always did always would
so when they hit pogey I said "Hurray!"

And they went for more and that was fine
I had mine, I didn't mind
I went to bed early and slept well

I dreamt of no deficit, no taxes, a budget well-balanced
sitting square like a couple of steaks on a butcher's scale

And my Chevy was a Buick and February in
Florida and life and all and all as neat and trim
as Karen Walker's desk in grade six

      ★ ★ ★

Then the plant closed and Marg stayed home

And Ma couldn't make it on her own and moved in
and took to fighting with Marg

Then at the office they trimmed the fat
and there was a strike
but I had my mortgage and my family
I didn't go out

And they lightened the ship and moved south
and I was redundant and didn't
and was home

So I looked around and called on my friends
but they were all slinging burgers or pumping gas
and mostly doing lots of nothing like me

And I was home with Marg and Ma
and we argued
and they bitched

So to clear it all up we went for a drive
and the car broke down and we had no cash
and there was no bus
so we walked

And we were home

And we couldn't pay the cable
so the screen went blank
and we argued
and we bitched

And Marg ran up a bill so the phone went too

And pogey ran out

So we pulled up our socks, we weren't done
we trudged off to Welfare
and there was a phone on a wall with a slot for your quarter

And a line a half-mile long
people huffing and stomping in the cold

And Ma took ill

And we went to the hospital
but that was credit cards only
and ours were all cancelled

And I wrote a letter
and copied it over

One for my MP another for the PM
another for my MPP and one for the Premier
and another for the mayor and on down the line

And we didn't have a phone so we
didn't have a fax
so I tramped all over town
and there weren't any stamps and no box

And Marg tried singing on streetcorners
and I made wire toys
and the competition was tough
and we lost more than we made

And we stayed home
and we bitched
and we drank

And we didn't make the payments
and were evicted

        ★ ★ ★

Ma died
Marg is gone

The kids've moved to the States
he's doing seven no parole
she's working nights

And the little one?
she married into money
—there's still some around somewhere I suppose—
and wouldn't know her old Dad

And as for me I can't say I know what street this is
or what town
but its effing freezing so it must be home
or thereabouts

The snow's blowing up, the lights have gone out
it's time to lie down
sleep till the thaw

MILES

Ignore the name,
you'll never say it right—
call me Miles, instead, like the jazzman
and focus, please,
on my accomplishments

I am Canadian
I am a nuclear physicist,
B.Sc. from Astrakhan,
Ph.D., Moscow,
12 years beyond the Urals

I attended many congresses,
was invited to Geneva,
had coffee with Sakharov
and was beaten up for the pleasure

I speak four languages,
I've published three books of poetry,
all unfortunately in a language
no one cares about anymore

There were many physicists in my country,
many poets—

I know Microsoft, I know Java,
I understand OOP
and have stayed countless nights till dawn
debugging C++

Focus on my accomplishments

Call me Miles. Please,
every journey must begin somewhere

MY GRANDFATHER'S LIFE
IN TWENTY-THREE LINES, APPROXIMATELY
for Maurice Rigaux 1904-2000

It was a long, rambling affair
though not uneventful

My brother died,
my sister went to Paris;
I painted houses, roadsigns,
whatever brought in a franc

I married,
a foreigner of sorts—she spoke French imperfectly—
fathered two daughters, no sons

I idled through the phoney war,
was surrendered,
threw potatoes when I could to those poor Russians,
escaped

My wife was dead,
my daughters somewhere in Vichy

When we got home at last we sold the house
and they emigrated

In August 1987 with my grandsons,
grown and foreign and herding home,
I played pétanque

And in Normandy now the graveyard
is hidden
even from the sea

Not Darkness, Not Light

Do not speak to me of darkness,
of darkness or roaring light

In darkness are no echoes,
in light no sounds at all

Speak to me rather
of the slate-black river

And the willow
stepping suddenly from the fog

January, 6 p.m.

It had not been a good day,
a walk might help, my dad had said

So we went out and I took his hand,
and showed him how the air was full of diamonds,
and the snow, how it was piled along the street
so high I was afraid to climb the heaps alone

We kicked some lumps and ran a bit,
and in our boots as big as breadloaves
it seemed we made no noise
There are days like this, he said

Days like what? I wondered, but didn't ask,
and trudged on beside, to the top of Putman Road

LULU'S POEM

Father says I'm always late
Mother says she hates to wait
so wash my hands and brush my teeth
and get in the car and hurry up
and she's fed up so why's
she have to say it twice
and twice again

Teacher says I'm much too slow
I'm nice, she says, but in the clouds
or on the moon, or in the stars, or somewhere else
and sent me off to see the principal and learn
to wake up and look sharp and
listen!
so she doesn't have to say it twice
and twice again

I like to touch things and to smell
I like to see plants grow, and animals
I want to know how can the wind
push clouds and why waves are waves
and why it is you're big and I am small
and ants are even less

I like to read some words a hundred times
because they make a special sound
and count the dots in pictures and
think of all the colours that are there
and count them too, twice
and twice again

I like to feel the way things feel
especially the ones that squish and burp
or snap and creak and crunch
or watch a sidewalk crack for alien life
or worms
and think some more about such things—
though when I think I usually forget

I know I'm late
I know I'm slow

but I'm just a kid

46

SENTIMENTAL POEM FOR MAHA

You'll just have to imagine
this is a love poem
just have to look in your own
heart. You know
I'm no good at that sort of thing
no good at love poems

I wrote a few, sure
but that was long ago
was another time
another life, that was ...
something that wasn't

And you would want a real one
a real love poem, something
perfumed, polished
intricate as a ghazal
as the tile-work on a Persian mosque
smooth as the inside of an oyster shell

So you'll just have to imagine
that this is a love poem
that it's like a Fairouz song
like her best, for Beirut
only more so

The longing, the nostalgia
unadulterated by music, untouched by voice
by an aging singer,
by violinists sweating through yet another encore
their thoughts already on a nargilé
on a glass of arak

You'll have to imagine the words—
where the words take you
an olive grove, a night among the cypresses
a stone village

You'll have to imagine
the barred courtyard of your school
your grandmother outside

A ripe watermelon
the blue blue Mediterranean

A HOTEL IN ALEPPO

In a hotel in Aleppo
by a window upon a courtyard

In a hotel in Aleppo
under a fan idly circling,
and someone outside
coughing or crying

In a hotel in Aleppo
within sight of the citadel
and the mountain

in a room

In a hotel in Aleppo
we pulled back at last
the sheets of our years

Worn and wrong to the touch,
soiled with love
and anger and ennui

In a hotel in Aleppo
in a room

With a fan idly circling
and someone outside
coughing or crying

We said,
"It's time to go"

In a hotel in Aleppo
by a window upon a courtyard

the night swollen with jasmine,
the moon in a fountain

To Moscow, Without Losses

Here it was an item on the morning news

We'd won, the radio said,
the dam had burst, the wall collapsed,
and freedom they said it was,
was flooding east beyond Berlin

So fast it travelled
the television crews were unable to keep up

By the time the first rumours reached us
Budapest had been engulfed
and Bratislava

Icons were defaced, monuments toppled,
but there was little time to fill the streets,
and only moderate rejoicing

East to Warsaw, east to Prague,
east to Tallinn and Kiev,
east to Moscow, without losses,
and the Urals

Workers were caught unawares at tramstops,
children found their teachers in a muddle,
and a pensioner and veteran somewhere unpronounceable
committed suicide

Freedom they said it was

In a matter of hours it had rippled across ten time zones,
washed through Tashkent,
blue Samarkand and Baikal .

Though on account of the time difference
it was not until the next calendar day
that Vladivostok was officially reached

The echo boomed across the Sea of Japan,
and major capitals of the Americas and Europe were annoyed
by a not insignificant increase in smog

Freedom they said it was
though the stock exchanges registered hardly a quiver

Hong Kong and Shanghai were outwardly unaffected,
in Lagos and Bangkok the weather was unbearable,
and the usual number of flights left Mumbai International

In Christchurch the wind was cold for the season,
though on the South Island the sheep,
and the penguins further south still
did not notice

No one was ready for this, said a pundit,
no one prepared

Though strangely,
and perhaps also because television crews
had time to set up

In Sarajevo the effect
was almost immediate

THIS YEAR, 2001

In this year, named after a movie
and not yet quite ended,
many things happened

A few hundred species of mollusk went extinct

A submarine sank somewhere off Murmansk,
and while the media and military
agonized over the probability
of nuclear contamination,
300 metres beneath the ice
the crew had a few days
to watch themselves die

In Saudi Arabia and Texas
executions continued as per routine
and the commandment of the Book

Amnesty International published reports

The UN passed resolutions

In Silicon Valley speculators were shocked and chagrinned,
and executives began layoffs—
these were tough decisions, they said

Cows went mad in England and Scotland and Wales,
and governments took measures

The Balkans continued being the Balkans

The American president
provoked an incident with China

Palestinians threw stones,
a few brought guests uninvited
to collective suicide events

They were thanked as per routine,
with rocket bombs and bulldozers

In Québec many were arrested

A boatload of refugees, shipwrecked then rescued,
was not allowed to land in Australia

An Airbus without engines visited the Azores

Other planes brought the wars home
to Washington and New York

A woman on Rideau Street
lay in the door of a bank
and howled for clean sheets and breakfast

This Morning Precisely, the Barbarians

This morning, precisely,
the barbarians arrived

Though not as we had imagined,
not dark and hungry,
nor blond and large either,
or full of swagger

I saw some, I thought,
descend from an airplane;
they looked like my father and myself

Some brought their women,
though they were not pretty

But mostly it was economists and the press

They were exceedingly polite,
not at all the louts
we had come to expect

Though except for the whores
unwilling to make truck
with the local population

A later report had them huddled
in a hotel of moderate luxury,
like gentlemen at cards
trading destinies

But of this as well
we could not be certain

Barricades and policemen
obstructed the view

How War Was Declared

We were busy, I suppose,
with other matters

Our mortgages, our in-laws
that unfortunate and sudden decline of the TSE,
the Nikkei and the rest

We hardly noticed
when our ships put to sea
and our jets shrieked off beyond the horizon—

To settle things, our leaders said

The enemy, now we all know,
has slipped hidden onto our shores

Yesterday I saw a message
he, or someone just like him,
had posted to a wall

"Under the rubble of my house
rats ate the face of my child"

My Life as a Tourist

In Shiraz, famous for poetry and gardens,
I found a blue tile beside a mosque

But I did not go to Teheran;
the streets there, I was told,
are dusty and sad

Hong Kong was unexpected;
the people are friendly
and the trees very foreign,
but it was difficult to sleep

In Windsor and London I was unemployed,
in Providence I dug graves,
and in Toronto I started on Bay Street

In Richer, at the edge of the prairie,
the water was red and tasted of mud

Montreal was mostly confusing,
Kimiko said: "The best wives are from Kyoto"
but I did not take up the offer

Valparaíso was all stairs,
and the women were lovely

I did not see Beckett
read a book in the Luxembourg,
but I know he did that once

Did anyone mention the Porte de Pantin,
how at night it looks like a fairground
about to be closed?

I was arrested in Yabello,
in Erbil as well,
but Yabello was worse

In Oulu a granny knitting at the station
sent me to a whorehouse,
when all I wanted was a room

In Muonio I did not speak Swedish

It was 50 below in Karelia,
but the war was over

And at the Finland Station we were fortunate .
and shabby enough to melt into the crowd

In Iqaliut I watched the sun roll along the horizon,
and in Awasa I rowed into a rainstorm

From Dhaka to Mombasa
I shivered under the monsoon

But in Dar es Salaam I was able to describe
red dhows and white houses against a green sea

We concluded in Damascus, called Shaam,
with coffee and a fortune teller,
and the day falling into the mountain behind us

I still have my blue tile,
but I have yet not been to Teheran,
sweet Lisbon

Or seen the stars floating
over lonely Dushanbé

The Price of Transmigration

When at last I entered the House of the Lord
few bargains were left

In fact, most items had been recently repriced

In immaculate glass cases
locked and under surveillance
by angels in dark uniforms and caps
were the fortunate lives

Beside each an elegant brochure
listed its attributes
and concluded:
"by Appointment Only"

Angels behind counters
adjusted their lipstick and chatted,
but apparently could not hear me
when I asked for advice

It seems the best wares
were reserved for friends of the management
or priced beyond reach

I needed something more common

On the topmost floor
in a bargain bin by the cafeteria
I finally found something I thought I could afford

I handed it to a golden-haired angel
who weighed up a portion,
her thumb on the scale

"You'll need credit," she said,
"That's downstairs"

I followed the signs all the way down
and queued up

At wicket 6 the clerk was formal
"We're obliged to give you credit," he said,
"but considering the present market and your past
the terms won't be good"

He adjusted his glasses,
pulled a long feather from his wing,
cut a nib and scribbled in a ledger

"No receipt?" I asked,
but he was busy already with a tall man in plaid

I climbed the stairs
and found my way back to pick up my portion

In my hands it was smaller
than it had seemed on the scale

I tried to ask the angel for water,
something to keep it from wilting,
but she was having a coffee and smoke
and ignored me completely

Sheltering my purchase
from elbows and unseemly stares
I made my way to the exit

The Lord was working the cash,
a pencil behind his ear

"Sign here," he said
and handed me a paper the size of a bedsheet,
all in fine print

But the words: "No Refunds. No Returns"
were clear enough

"You're overdrawn already," he said,
"you took your time,
and interest does compound"

I emptied my wallet onto the counter:
small bills, a family photo,
two lottery tickets

"I'll just hold on to these," smiled the Lord,
"and your clothes as well, if you don't mind"

An Elephant Dies
in the Valley of the Po

How wrong I was

When we wound our way at last
through the passes south
I thought I was going home

How different this river

How many miles did I walk
to come to this place?

How many leagues since I was calved
by the Third Cataract in the Land of Kush?

The drivers were not amused,
they had a caravan to move
before the heat came north

I clutched my mother's tail
and followed her to the delta,
then west

To the edge of the earth,
the long trek to the snow

How cold the sun here

When we came down from the passes
I thought I was going home

What a sight I was,
an African monster
lumbering out of the mountains

How they ran before my trumpet!

How different this river

Where does the brown water go?
Why are the trees without leaves?
When will the sun become warm?

How wrong I was

Magpies poke about in the mess
Gleaners quarrel over corpses

A spotted dog comes to sniff,
trots away into the fog

Writers write about the world in which they live. Here is a map to mine.

At the End of Triana
Triana is a pedestrian street in Las Palmas de Gran Canaria. Paseo and barranco are two words that have passed (though incompletely) from Spanish into English. They are, respectively, a pedestrian street and a canyon. Juan Negrín, who was from Las Palmas, was the last president of the Second Spanish Republic (1931-39).

Attila József's Last Poem
The Hungarian poet Attila József wrote "Epitaph for A Spanish Campesino" after the fall of Irun in the Civil War. He later threw himself under a freight train.

EPITAPH FOR A SPANISH CAMPESINO

The Fascists called me up and I went.
No, I didn't run away, I didn't desert,
I was afraid, you see, I would have been shot.
I was afraid, that's why I went,
why I fought there against liberty, against justice,
there with the army at the gates of Irun.
There where death found me anyway.

Brunete
Brunete is a village near Madrid. It was the site of terrible fighting during the Civil War. Many Canadians were killed there defending the Spanish Republic.

Cádiz
Dragon trees are native to the Canaries and a few other islands in the Atlantic. Their red sap is said to resemble blood.

Córdoba
Córdoba was the jewel of Ummayad Spain; Moslems, Jews and Christians lived there in relative harmony until the very Catholic Reconquista (Reconquest) got there. It is not close to the sea. The Great Mosque of Córdoba is a marvel of Islamic architecture. Maïmonides was one of the greatest philosophers and physicians of the Middle Ages; he was born in Córdoba in 1135. Lorca was not from Córdoba, but from Granada, which is also in Andalusia, but he wrote a poem about Córdoba. The AVE is Spain's high speed train, which runs from Madrid to Seville via Córdoba. The Guadalquivir (in Arabic "Great River") also goes from Córdoba to Seville and continues to the Atlantic. Abbas ben Farras did what the poem says he did.

De Falla at the Police Station
The composer Manuel de Falla was born in Cádiz. He was living in Granada when Lorca was killed there in the early days of the Civil War. He was one of the few who had the courage to protest the murder of the poet.

An Elephant Dies in the Valley of the Po
The Po is a river in Italy. Kush was the land south of Ancient Egypt. Carthage fought Rome for control of the Western Mediterranean.

For Señor Layton
In "Brief Letter to Cervantes" Irving Layton describes an unfortunate encounter he had with a Castilian cheese merchant. A duro is the common term for five pesetas (about five cents). Spaniards still quote small sums in duros: 20 duros for 100 pesetas, for example. The poet Quevedo is best known for his merciless critique of Spanish society.

Guernica
Guernica is a Basque town. It was destroyed during the Spanish Civil War by Hitler's and Mussolini's aviators honing their skills.

Half-Day in Madrid
The Prado and the Reina Sofía are museums. The Puerta del Sol is a
popular spot in Madrid. Espronceda is a street.

Hendaya
Hendaya is the border crossing between France and Spain on the Atlantic
coast. Austerlitz is the station in Paris for trains to the south-west, and
Spain.

Letter from the Málaga Road
A Heinkel is German warplane. During the Spanish Civil War, Norman
Bethune, 'Beth' to some of his friends, set up the world's first mobile
blood transfusion service, the Servicio Canadiense de Transfusión de
Sangre, for the Republic. He witnessed the massacre of civilians fleeing
Málaga after it fell to the Fascists and described what he saw in a pam-
phlet, *The Crime on the Road: Málaga-Almería.* Afraid the capital would fall
early in the war, the government of the Republic moved itself to Valencia
when rebel forces were at the gates of Madrid.

Miles
Miles Davis played the trumpet and invented be-bop and cool. Andrei
Sakharov was a Soviet physicist who helped build the hydrogen bomb,
then fell afoul of the authorities. Java and C++ are programming lan-
guages. OOP is an acronym for Object Oriented Programming, which is
supposed to be better than procedure-based programming.

My Grandfather's Life in Twenty-Three Lines, Approximately
Pétanque is a game played by throwing large steel balls at a tiny wooden
ball. Pastis is a drink created especially for drinking when playing
pétanque.

Orwell's Dream
Orwell wrote of his time on the Aragón front and of his desire to drink
coffee in Huesca in *Homage to Catalonia.* The Army of Africa was the
Spanish colonial army These troops earned a reputation as fierce fighters
and cruel conquerors.

Sentimental Poem for Maha
A ghazal is classical form of Arabic poetry. Fairouz is a popular Arabic singer. A nargilé is a water pipe, and arak is a sweet alcoholic drink similar to pastis.

This Same War Once Again
Mac-Paps was the short form for the Canadian Mackenzie-Papineau Battalion in the International Brigades during the Spanish Civil War. Mercedes is a common name for Spanish women. In this case, however, Mercedes refers to the popular automobile.

Two Men, Honest and True
According to Webster's a hidalgo is "a member of the lower nobility of Spain." Holland isn't the only place with windmills; there are many in La Mancha. Rocinante is Don Quijote's horse, Dulcinea his lady.

ACKNOWLEDGEMENTS

Many thanks for their patience and support to Rebecca Leaver, Seymour Mayne, Susan Robertson and Ramesh Waghmare, and especially to Mark Frutkin, who has tirelessly read and critiqued this and many other manuscripts—many times.

Some of the poems in this collection have been published previously, sometimes in earlier versions, in *Alba*, *Bywords*, *Cinquefoil* (Ottawa, 2003), *Epitaph for a Good Canadian* (Ottawa, 1998), *Sealed in Struggle* (Madrid, 1995), *The Trumpeter* and *When the Mongols Return* (Oakville, 1994).